My Count

My

My Words

Edited by

Dr Marion Kickett

& Tracey Kickett

Copyright © Marion Kickett, 2023
Published: 2023 byLeschenault Press
Leschenault, Western Australia
ISBN: 9781922670939 - Paperback Edition
**

Cover Design by Brittany Wilson | Brittwilsonart.com

We would like to dedicate this book in memory of our old people who came before us.

Our Grandfather Thomas Kickett - Dajar
Grandmother Josephine Blurton
Grandfather Herbert Kickett
Our Father George Kickett Senior
Our Mother Pearl Kickett nee Narkle Brown
Uncle Walley Kickett
Auntie Glady Narkle
Uncle Billy Blurton/Kickett
Uncle Reginal Kickett

We are ever so grateful to have been raised on Barladong country where we belong. As was our father, our grandfather Dajar, our great grandfather – Yombich, our great, great grandfather William Thomas Kickett - Younigell, our great, great, great grandfather Cowitch – the first Native assistant policeman in York 1842.

We are privileged to have had numerous oral stories handed down to us by our father and his sisters Nellerine also known as Uboney Yarran nee Kickett and Pauline Narkle nee Kickett.

Introduction

This collection of personal stories grew out of a series of workshops conducted by Marion Kickett and Tracey Kickett during The York Festival 2022. The workshops were part of a broader program of cultural tours conducted by Marion and Tracey; both the workshops and tours were supported by Healthway, through their Act Belong Commit program.

But as Marion and Tracey explain in the following interview, this way of working was not ideal for many potential participants, and so the program was extended beyond the festival, both in terms of time and location. In other words, it was clear Marion and Tracey would have to "hit the road" in order to collect more stories.

The result is, to my mind, just the beginning of a longer project and a larger collection of stories. Because many Aboriginal people, while accustomed to "yarning", are not used to telling their stories with publication in mind. There is a certain natural reticence. Marion and Tracey are to be congratulated for gently encouraging the participants to share their stories with us.

Bearing this in mind, it is understandable that Marion and Tracey, in this first collection, would start with themselves and their immediate and extended family, and friends. Not only was this the path of least resistance; once published, other members of WA's aboriginal community would hopefully see the value in such a project and be inspired to share their own stories in like fashion. To the benefit of us all.

The stories – autobiography, memoir, prose poetry, life sketches, evocative fragments, yarns: they can be difficult to categorise! – are often short and deceptively simple. Many are entertaining, and very funny – the tale of Billy the Kid being one such example. Others, such as those which touch on growing up on the York reserve or giving birth in less than ideal conditions, are moving and poignant.

Then there are the distinctive voices, which come through the writing, and which we have tried to preserve during the editing process. Perhaps your ears will be offended by grammatical solecisms and strange turns of phrase. One has to remember these stories are part of a rich tradition of oral storytelling, as vital and alive today as it has always been. And that individual voices should be honoured for their uniqueness, not refined and repackaged for mass consumption.

This is not social history. This is not anthropology. This is the sharing of story, pure and simple.

Will Yeoman
Artistic Director
The York Festival

An interview with
Marion and Tracey Kickett

Will Yeoman (WY): This beautiful collection of personal stories originated in a series of storytelling workshops held during The York Festival 2022, but soon grew beyond that! Can you tell me how the project evolved?

Marion Kickett (MK): Setting aside time and asking individuals to come and write their story both Tracey and I knew was not going to work. It's not what noongars do. What we had to do is go to the individual or invite the individual to come to our home and have a yarn about their connection to York.

During the festival, two individuals came but did not sit down and write; they preferred to go home and write their story. Of the two, only one wrote her story. We yarned with everyone about their connection to York, explaining what we meant. Some individuals thought about their connection and what their story would be. It was easier to record them telling their story and then type the story. We would then read the story aloud to the individual, who then informed us what they wanted to change or leave. This process worked well for most participants. Some participants typed their stories and we worked with them to edit their story.

For me it was allowing more time to let individuals think about a story and then be happy to share. Both Tracey and I were asked to write extra stories about an individual that was related to us, and we knew well. I agreed to share the story of William Kickett (Billy the Kid) as told to me by my dad. Uncle Billy's 10-year-old great grandson, whom I had never met before, asked me very excitedly if I could tell the story about his great grandfather using a real gun and real bullets in a cowboy game. He wanted the full story as told to me by my dad who was his great grandfather's older brother.

So, time had to be given and when this happened things evolved into us receiving beautiful, deep and meaningful stories that we could add to in some cases. The stories are all so different.

Tracey Kickett (TK): What Marion mentioned above is very true. We did complete a flyer and handed it out a couple of weeks before the story telling sessions during the York Festival. We had five Aboriginal people turn up and only one wrote their story. The other four wanted to go away and think a bit more about a story. Two of the four did end up writing a story.

We used every opportunity to ask Aboriginal people who had a connection to York if they would like to share a story. Most we asked did want to and some just refused.

The process of yarning was used with each person. Before recording the story, yarning was a very effective tool as it helped in relaxing and calming the storyteller's nerves, and helped bring back memories for them that provided more depth to their story and allowed much humour to be shared and enjoyed by all. I found the whole experience really fun and learnt so much about different storytellers.

WY: What were some of the challenges in working with so many different people from across the state? What were the joys?

MK: The challenges in working with different people was some had left York and visited occasionally. While some others were not from York but had a connection by coming to live in York and staying.

Individuals who were not Noongar but living in Noongar country felt they didn't have a story or a connection. We needed to make them feel included.

We needed to yarn with each individual and tease out a story that connected them to York. Some found this difficult to do but after yarning about their lives where they lived? who they were related to? Why they lived in York? Such challenges needed to be addressed.

The joys for me were listening to a younger person yarn about a loved one who had passed away and then share a story their father had told them about their grandparents. It is confirmation that the traditional storytelling is continuing.

TK: I totally agree. Some individuals are natural storytellers, like Aron Slater. Some found the yarning and then telling their story provided much healing for them. Others needed more prompting and a few questions asked to elaborate on the story. Yarning has no time limit, and the process can be very time-consuming. This was a challenge as most Aboriginal people love yarning.

WY: Why do you think encouraging people to tell their life stories is important for themselves and for the rest of the community?

MK: Telling the stories for themselves was healing for some individuals even though it was challenging for them, too. We supported an individual by saying they did not have to talk about when they were taken. Their reply was they wanted to talk about it, as it was a part of their life.

Telling their story helped individuals to connect to country connect to each other and affirm and reaffirm where they belonged. This being so important to an individual's identity.

Telling their life stories is so important to the rest of the community as it is a way of sharing with the community. The rest of the community will be strengthened by individual stories. Strong role models are very important in communities along with having pride in oneself and one's culture and community.

TK: I just wanted to add that we do not want these stories to be lost or never told. We want them to be passed on to future generations about their family, extended family and individuals within the Aboriginal community of York and surrounding areas.

WY: Oral storytelling is central to Australian Aboriginal culture. Do you think this has changed in modern times, with modern technology providing so many alternatives and distractions?

MK: No, I still believe oral stories are a major part of our storytelling. Many Aboriginal people still like to sit and yarn and tell stories. This has come through in collecting these stories.

TK: Oral stories are a very important aspect of Aboriginal culture, history, and kinship. Oral stories are Aboriginal people's recording of everything along with song and dance. The way our culture was preserved since Dreaming. Using modern technology ensures that these stories can be shared with the wider Aboriginal community and old ways are preserved.

WY: What do you think other Aboriginal people can learn from these stories? What about non-Aboriginal people? What can they learn?

MK: Other Aboriginal people can learn the importance of sharing their stories for the next generations. The positive impact on many other Aboriginal people. Aboriginal people who do not have a lived experience of Aboriginal life can learn about some of their family and life practices.

TK: It will encourage other Aboriginal people to be proud of who they are and where they come from. How strong, clever, resilient and proud their ancestors and old people were in their different language groups and dialects.

MK: For non- Aboriginal people there is a lot they can learn, as many of these stories are truth telling in a gentler way. This is history for many people. Some of the past government policies are filtered through some of the stories. How individuals coped, survived, and overcame racism.

Non-Aboriginal people will learn about the importance of humour in Aboriginal people's lives. Many stories are very comical.

TK: Non-Aboriginal people will learn firsthand from individuals about their connection to York and what were special memories for some Aboriginal people.

WY: What is your hope for this collection?

MK: My hope for this collection is to educate and inspire the next generations of family members. I hope this collection will be seen as truth telling in a positive way.

TK: We want this to be a book that is treasured by future generations of Aboriginal people of York and surrounding areas, where they can share with their families the beautiful stories within. For non-Aboriginal people, a book that opens a doorway for them to connect with Aboriginal people currently living or who used to live in York. Most Aboriginal people would never share such stories with non-Aboriginal people. So it is a great privilege to read these stories.

Legend of the Two Hills in York
as told by
George Kickett (Senior) Deceased

(Used as the basis for Two Mountains Dreaming, the opening event of The York Festial 2022)

There are two big hills in York. The biggest is Walwalling (Mt Bakewell), which means "place of weeping". The other is Wongborel (Mt Brown), which means "sleeping woman".

Now there's a reason for the two hills to have these names. The Noongars gave these names to the hills because of what happened a long time ago. This is the Dreaming…

Years and years ago, one family of Noongars came to live here in York. They cleared some of the trees away and burned the bushes and the grass. Every year they would burn the grass and when new grass would grow the kangaroos would come and eat the sweet new grass. The Noongars would kill the kangaroos for food and they would use the skins to keep themselves warm cause it could get cold in the valley of the two hills.

Anyway, as time went by the family got bigger and there were too many people living in the valley. The old man said to his two youngest sons, "I want you to go and see what food you can get up in the hills."

The youngest sons left early in the morning and started climbing the hills. They came back with lots of different types of foods. They told their father that there was plenty to eat in the hills.

The old man decided to send his two youngest sons and their wives to live on the two hills. They had many children and grandchildren.

Time went on and the old man was ready to die, so he sent for his sons and their children and grandchildren. Down from the hills they all came to see the old man. They all played sports, games and danced around the fires and hunted together and all had a big feed. The old man watched the games, he watched them all dance around the fire, and he ate the food that was caught for him and then he died with all his family around him.

Every year at the same time the hills Noongars and the valley Noongars would meet in the valley.

They would dance around the fires, play games and hunt and eat together. For many years they did this.

Then one year, something wrong happened, one young fulla whose name was Wundig came down from the hills, he has *moorditj marts* (good legs) and he could run fast and was a good hunter. It was soon time for him to marry the *yorga* (girl) he was promised to, she was from over the other side of the hills. But he didn't want to.

Wundig wanted to marry Wilura who was from the valley people. This was wrong, because they were related. They decided to take off together.

The valley Noongars thought Wilura was living with Wundig up in the hills and the hills Noongars thought Wundig was living with Wilura down in the valley. The valley Noongars went looking for Wilura up in the hills. The hills Noongars told the valley Noongars that they didnt know where the two young fullas were. The valley Noongars wouldn't believe the hill Noongars and a big fight started.

The hills Noongars were too good on their own land in the hills and a lot of valley Noongars were killed. The valley Noongars still left alive looked up and saw more hill Noongars coming from the other hill. There was too many of them, so the valley Noongars went back down to the valley and called on their *mubarn* man (clever fulla) and asked him to use his *mubarn*.

As the other hill people came over the big hill and down the slope they were turned into *balgas* (black boy bushes). To this day you can see them standing still on the big hill. The *mubarn* man then turned his *mubarn* on Wundig and Wilura and they both died. *He's a law man. They broke the law and have to be killed.*

Wundig's *karnya* (shame) would stay on Walwalling ("place of weeping") and his *yorga* (girls). Wilura's *karnya* was sent to the other hill that he called Wongborel ("sleeping woman"). The *mubarn* man said that Wundig and Wilura would never meet again until the two hills came together, and he made the river run between them. This is how it still is today.

The *mubarn* man turned back to Walwalling and said that if any Noongar climbed the hill they had to climb to the top. If they didn't make it to the top, then someone in their family would die.

So if you are going to climb Walwalling today, make sure you can climb it to the top!

My Connection to York

I was born in Wiluna WA and lived most of my life in the Northwest. I grew up on a sheep and cattle station named Milgun, north of Meekatharra. My father was the head stockman and windmill repair man, and my mother was the cook, both at the homestead and out in the mustering camp.

My parents owned Pingandy Station and when they retired, my husband and I ran the station for a while before we sold up and came to live down here. We arrived in the Avon Valley at an area called Westdale, about 30 km southwest of Beverley, in 1984.

We purchased a small 100 acre/40 hectare farm that we cropped and ran sheep. I sometimes visited York with my family to do shopping, attend the Jazz Festival and other activities. I brought my children to York to attend discos and inter school sporting events. A few years after I arrived, I started work at the Beverley District High School as a teacher's aide.

While working there I studied and gained a teaching degree. As a teacher's aid, I helped the (mainly indigenous) children with their lessons.

I assisted the art teacher with setting up the art material for lessons and then helping with the lessons. I helped council children who had problems within the school. I tried to attend any meeting where the children had to see the principal or deputy principal. I went on school excursions, inter school sports and cross-country events. I usually had care of the indigenous children.

On faction school sports days, swimming, track, and field events I would be in the tent area for a particular faction, helping ensure the children were ready for their events. I was president of the Aboriginal School Fund for the school. Our committee met and made decisions on where this grant money should be spent to assist indigenous children with their education. The principal was a member of the committee and encouraged our programmes.

We often had well-known Aboriginal identities come to our school to give talks/workshop etc. Artist and cultural speakers were often involved. We concentrated on sports people as they were the role models the children preferred. I usually greeted the guests and introduced them to the teachers and children. However, I made one very embarrassing blunder when this very nice young man arrived, and I asked him who he was. He said he was Chris Lewis and I asked him what he did. He told me he played football, and I asked him what team he played for. Yes, really I did. When he told me I quickly took him to the sports teacher and then disappeared because I was so embarrassed.

I liaised with the families on school matters and often discussed the future for their children, as well as vocational opportunities that could be investigated. I came to know families in town like the Mourishes, Ugles, Kicketts and many others. I met elder and well-known artist Dennis Kickett. I taught his children Michelle and Dennis, and now Michelle and I both live in York!

My daughter, Bindi, joined the Beverley Horse and Pony Club and we participated in many events in York. I worked as a volunteer gear checker at many inter club and Avon Zone events. Controversial decisions had to be made that did not please everyone, but that was my job. Due to a dispute with a York family, I was not treated very well. I wrote expressing my feelings about the situation to the Zone committee and they passed my letter onto Head Office. The result was a very thick folder with strict rules for gear checking in every category.

I had spent many years in the north as a teacher. When I returned, I first worked full-time in Beverley and then part-time as a teacher in York three days a week as one of the art teachers. After I retired, I sometimes worked as a relief teacher in York, Quairading, and Beverley. My husband died in 2004 and I stayed on at the farm in the Westdale until 2017. I sold the farm that year and moved to York to live.

I have attended the Seniors Mobility Group for exercise activities. I joined Probus and enjoyed the many guest speakers and outings that this group offered. In 2020 Covid 19 closed everything down and I have not returned to these clubs. I attended the Aboriginal Art and Craft group that met weekly at the rooms next door to the Post office. I am also a member of the Googala Bilya group. I attend the York Aware Group that meet weekly at the park near the river. I have been attending the York Peace Park Markets and the Medieval Markets for many years, selling dog coats and crocheted tea towels. I enjoy living in York and all the activities it offers and the many friends I have made here.

Marjorie Kirkoff

Philip Narrier

I left Moore and came to York when I was 16 with my dad's sister and her husband. We were coming to see my other aunty who lived in York on the reserve. My aunty and uncle told me they were not going back to Moore, so I had to stay in York. I didn't mind because I really loved my aunty and uncle in York. I met my wife who was living with her family on the reserve: she was my uncle's niece. So, my first cousins were also my wife's first cousins.

When I was asked to be in the play Two Mountains Dreaming for the opening of The York Festival, I felt honoured. This was my uncle George Kickett's story about the two mountains. I remember Uncle telling me this story when my brother Neil come to visit. Neil wanted to climb the biggest hill in York. Aunty Pearl told Neil to talk to Uncle George about climbing hills in York. So that's what Neil and I did.

When I first heard the story being read aloud, I cried. I remembered my uncle telling my brother and me about the story when we were just teenage boys. He told us to climb all the way to the top and to make sure we did.

I played for the York Football Club when I first moved here and stayed for a few years. I always came back to York to visit family and attend funerals. As Noongars that's what we do. Pat and I lived in York for a few years raising some of our grannies here.

I have a strong connection to York, having lived there for a big part of my life. I have some wonderful memories of the town. It was good to come back and spend this time here doing the play for the festival.

Philip Narrier

Wal-Waaliny (Mt Bakewell)

Growing up in York I would always look at Wal-Waaliny (Mt Bakewell)

To see what sort of day it was going to be.

Sunny, hot, cold, rain, cloudy, misty, or stormy,

No matter what, when I looked over my shoulder and saw Wal-Waaliny it was going to be a good day.

To see the beauty and the bush or *boodja* around it I knew in my heart this was my home, my *boodja* (land) a *moorditj* (good) place to be.

Walking out the door to go to school,

I see Wal-Waaliny it was going to be a good day.

Going for a drive with my family,

I see Wal-Waaliny it was going to be a good day.

Going for a ride on my bike to the river,

I see Wal-Waaliny it was going to be a good day.

In the winter standing in cold water up to my knees
looking for tadpoles near the railway line,

I see Wal-Waaliny it was going to be a good day.

There were times I would look at Wal-Waaliny and
think to myself how much it looked like a beautiful
big whale.

I see Wal-Waaliny it was going to be a good day.

Now I am older, when I go back to York to a place
where my family past, present and the

Future come from, I will always know in my heart

This was and always will be my home, my *boodja*
(land) a *moorditj* (good) place to be.

Especially when I see Wal-Waaliny

And know all is well.

Brenda (Jones) Larsen

Carol Kickett

My name is Carole Kickett. My connection with York is through my Kickett family.

My grandfather Herbert Kickett's brother, Tom Kickett, lived on the York Reserve. I remember my parents taking me there to visit our family in York on the reserve many times.

Coming from a big family and visiting more family in York I was told there were other family members with the same names. I was told there was another Janice and another Marion in York.

I also found out I had another uncle, Wally Kickett. There were other family there as well, but I didn't get to meet all of them. When these photos were taken, I remember Uncle George holding this little chubby girl. (Sorry, Mow!) I felt like holding her, but I was too scared. I didn't realise at the time, but it was Marion who he was holding.

I do remember the watermelons that we bought in York. Uncle George or Uncle Wally would come with us to see the two Chinese market gardeners. I'd never ever tasted watermelons like that, they were delicious and sweet, and you can't get watermelons like that now or ever.

Ten years after that visit I met Audrey Nettle, we started talking about our family and how we were related to each other. She told me about the family in York. From then on, my daughter Regina sister Janice and I visited our Kickett family in York. We lived in Redcliffe, and it wasn't far to go and see them.

Reginia and I spent many holidays up there with Janice (RIP), Marion, Donna (RIP) and Tracey. We would go to the swimming pool practically every day. It was so hot during the summer, so we spent most of our time at the swimming pool.

During this time, we also came to know Uncle George (RIP) and Aunty Pearle (RIP) a lot better. We also got to meet all my other aunties, uncles, and cousins.

I have some precious memories of spending time in York and would like to share these three photos that were taken when I was 12 years old, visiting my family that lived in York on the reserve.

Carol Kickett

Back row l-R Reginald Kickett, Wally Kickett(Cuballing)
Fred Hill, Wally Kickett (York) Fraser Kickett
Middle Row Brothers Tom and , Herbert Kickett.
Front Row Kelvin Kickett and Maurice Kickett
very front two children Graham Kickett and Alan Kickett
Taken on the York reserve at the front of Tom Kickett's
home

Backrow Carol Kickett (age 12) holding baby Karen Kickett,
Kelvin Kickett,
Rront row Natalie Hill, Jan Kickett (Cuballing) Allan Kickett,
Graham Kickett and Fred Hill junior. Photo taken on the
York reserve 1963

Front - Josephine Blurton holding bunch of grapes.
Back - Janice Kickett (4-Year-old York Janice Kickett)
Graham Kickett, Pearl Kickett and George Kickett (senior)
holding baby Marion Kickett (York Marion Kickett)
Photo taken on the York Reserve. 1963

Janice Kickett

My name is Janice Kickett. I live in Pingelly WA. As a child, I don't remember going to York with my mum, Irene Collard Woods Kickett (RIP), and my dad, Reginal Kickett (RIP).

Looking through old photos that were taken in York at the old reserve, there are my uncle Kelvin Kickett (RIP), my sister Carol Kickett holding baby Karen Kickett (RIP), Natalie Hill, me, Allan Tonkey Kickett (RIP), Graham Kickett and Fred Hill (JR). With all my cousins.

In my late teens we would travel to York from Redcliffe on the weekend and holidays to stay with Uncle George and Aunty Pearl and their children Janice (RIP), Marion, Tracey, and Donna Narkle (RIP). We and everyone else were welcome to stay for as long as we wanted. Aunty Pearl would cook us a feed of kangaroo and damper. Uncle George would tell us yarns of when he worked the land from sunrise to sunset doing clearing with blood sweat and tears. He said there was no machinery, just his bare hands.

We moved back to Pingelly in the late 70s. My dad was unable to get his hair cut in Pingelly or Narrogin. But one hairdresser in Northam would cut his hair. So, on his way to Northam to get his hair cut, he would stop off and see Uncle George and Aunty Pearle for a yarn and a cuppa. Sometimes he would catch up with other family as well.

One day Uncle George asked Dad, "Why don't you get your hair cut here in York?" Dad thought York was the same as Pingelly and asked, "Do they cut Noongar's hair here?" Uncle said, "Yes, Max will cut your hair. He would cut mine, but I don't have much hair to cut, not like you. I'll take you down to see Max when you finish your tea".

Dad went to York every 3 to 4 weeks to get his hair cut. He was a distinguished gentleman. Everything had to be done right and this included his hair. I believe this was from his time in the army. Dad fought in WW2.

When Uncle George passed, Dad went down and put a death notice in the newspaper.

Janice Kickett

Following the *bidi* (track) Stories of my mother's lands

Cooee… was the sound of my aunt's voice, echoing loudly through the trees as the wind propelled it forward. This was the familiar sound, that I'd grown up with on the *bidi* tracks, back home in York and Beverley. I am a mother and a loving grandmother, and the eldest daughter of Barladong Whadjuk, Gwen and Albert Corunna. Mum's parents were Gladys Bunchy Blurton née Bandry and John Blurton. This wise Aboriginal woman was born at a time when her families had to have permits to work and move across our *Noongar* lands. When these restrictions were relaxing, Mum married Dad and moved away in 1961.

York was never far from Mum's mind, and it is often said that when a person leaves home, they still carry Country in their heart. This being true for Mum, as she was a child of the bush. She'd often find solitude in walking with her children along the sandy bush tracks near her *Balga* home. Those *bidi* tracks have now vanished being replaced with a large noisy highway.

The *bidi* stories which Mum first remembered as a child became the precious gems she would share with me. Born 1938 in Beverley under the time of restrictions, Mum and her family made their home in the bush during her early childhood years. It wasn't unusual to live in the bush in those time, as our families would have welcomed distance from the Law Enforcers. Nana Gladys had a challenging life protecting her children from the white people's law. Traveling as a child in a horse and cart down the *bidi* tracks was Mum's way of life.

Two main waterways, the Beverley Dale River and the York Avon became the family runs. It was along these waterways, that captivating stories were told of the places they lived. Mum would often say that they were the last of the old bushies to go and live in York town. All the other families had either moved away or were living in town.

These *bidi* tracks would lead us through the bush. As a child I remembered, running, and playing around near the *balga* trees, hearing many family voices including Mum's gathered in conversation around the glowing fire. The breeze carried delicious smells of lamb chops into the bush. Many times, we'd search for bush foods, and Nanna Gladys would show us the big mushroom fields. We'd walk, yarn and run up the hills laughing as we gathered the large mushrooms that awaited us. Soon after, the frying pan would be sizzling in the open fire. Pans were filled to the brim with fresh mushrooms and melting butter. So delicious! It was the way of life. The ways in which our family lived on these old *bidi* tracks continued to be shared with us.

Stories of sleeping in the *mia mia* were told by Mum, who was astounded by her dad's traditional knowledge and building skills. Mum said sleeping in the *mia mia* was warm and comforting. She often shared her joyful stories.

The Avon River was another place the family stayed, and Mum loved to share how her little fingers felt in the slimy mud, whilst catching the *gilgies*. Sometimes if she was lucky, she'd escape a nip! At least that's what she told me. Buckets would be filled with *gilgies* and a large pot of boiling bubbling water would be on standby. Mum said, "It was good food straight from the river". This was one of the many *bidi* track stories.

Other times we'd travel the bitumen roads, heading first to Beverley before York. Mum knew the way, and again the stories flowed. As we passed the large farming estates, voices echoed the family names of the ones who'd given them work. Mum told us, "That our family had some gun shearers". I discovered that they were the best! Once at the Beverly Dale River Mum showed me the spot where they stayed by the river. It was a special site we called the 'naming place', because when Mum was a young girl, she was given her Noongar name by her Pop, Nurigal Robert Bandry.

I love traveling the *bidi* tracks, shouting out, "Cooee!" To be continued...

Excerpt from my book: *The Life of Gwen Corunna by Vanessa Maree Corunna a Barladong, Whadjuk, Palyku woman.*

Vanessa Corunna

My Noongar Birthplace at Miley Pool

I am a Noongar Elder now. And I am from York. My name is Dulcie Ponton. My maiden name is Blurton. I was born in 1946, in the month of July. Some people know me by the name Dolly. And I come from a family of many sisters and brothers. There is Gwen (RIP) the oldest, Muriel, Norma (RIP), Matt (RIP), Fred (RIP), Gail, Alan (RIP), Des, and Dianne. And we had two others, Beryl and Phillip who passed. York is where I was born and grew up.

Our family stayed at Des Moulton's farm and caught the bus to school because in my day there was the welfare and Dad John Blurton and Mum Gladys Blurton nee Bandry kept us in the bush.

I left school early and worked for Peter Carmichael, the policeman. His wife was a schoolteacher and when she'd come from school, she'd tell me, "Your brother Fred was playing up at school again."

I'd run home and tell Mum and Fred would be in trouble. I also worked on the Manning's Farm doing domestic chores. I'd get on my knees and scrub the floors. But I never got much pay.

We got a house on Grey Street in York with mum and dad and our big Noongar family.

When I became an adult, I found out through my birth certificate that I was born at Miley Pool in York, near the Avon River. I was so excited! When I got my birth certificate I said, "Well! I'm born at Miley Pool!"

I never asked Mum where I was born. And I never thought to ask her. My brother Matt said he was born there too. We were both born at Miley Pool. We were both the water babies.

Miley Pool must have been a place where our people camped. And it must have been a place for having the babies. I am not sure if any other women had babies at Miley Pool, but that was where Mum gave birth to two of her children.

When I came to York one time, I did tell a woman working for the Shire that I was born at Miley Pool, and I am not sure they knew that. I have my birth certificate.

We had Noongar women that would have helped Mum. I often think it would have been a beautiful place for birthing, with all the birds singing. If that place was just for the mothers, then it must have been one of our Noongar "birthing places".

York Barladong Whadjuk Elder
Dulcie Ponton

Happy Days at the River

My name is Sandra Narkle. I was born in York in 1951, on the veranda of the old hospital. I grew up on the York reserve. The first thing I can remember was being in the old tin shakes. But regardless of all that I was happy. I was a happy kid.

I remember being around my cousins and nans and pops old Grandmother Blurton. She was a darling old lady, she used to make us a lot of cakes and things. I can still see her face and Pop's. They were the happy days of being down at the river with my cousins and my sisters and brothers.

Having good times, happy times. That's what I must remember to do. Remember the happy days. The times spent swimming in the river. Looking for gilgies and turtle eggs and all that. We had an old tin down at the river we used to use to cook with.

I was happy because we had each other, and we were together. I had my two pops and two grans. I was lucky that they were there. Thinking about them now, it's so sad. But they was with us all the time.

Going to the pictures with Aunty Glady and Uncle Wally, they were the main two people to take us to the pictures, because you had to have adults with you at that time. Otherwise, we wouldn't get into the pictures.

The pictures were at the Town Hall and at the old picture theatre, the one where Fred ran into the door because the curtain was pulled across it. I think he was going to the toilet and the curtain was across it… anyway, he ran into the door.

When we used to go down to the river with our towels, I remember the hollow tree that we used to get dressed in it was like a dressing room.

Summertime, we were at the river all the time. There was the big pool and the little pool. The big pool was up near the bridge. We used to swim under water and see who could go under the water for the longest. Philip, he used to go a long way, he would go from one end to the other. He could hold his breath for a long time. Then we used to have a go, but we never got to where he did.

Looking at it now, it probably wasn't that far but when we were younger it looked a long way. We made a path because we used to walk to town by the river. It was the shortest way to town. Us kids would walk along the river. We even used to walk to the Sandy. That was like being on a beach, the sand was so clean. We didn't have much, but we were happy because we had each other. We never worried about snakes, and they never worried about us. We had our own swimming spots all the way from the reserve to town.

The little kids would swim in the cot in town once we got there. There was a diving board and one of my older cousins, he ran to dive into the water but he slipped. When he went into the water, everyone laughed and then when he came up out of the water everyone shut up.

I also remember down under the bridge Aunty Loma and her husband Uncle Lionel Wally, they used to sit under the middle bridge in town. I remember seeing it so clear, you could see him swimming in the water grabbing the turtles. Because Aunty Loma loved eating turtles and turtle eggs.

The river was so much better back then. It was cleaner, so much cleaner. So really, we had lovely times. They were such happy times. I remember catching the bus from the reserve and getting thrown off the bus because of Merle's fighting. We would line up and the bus would go flying past us and then we would have to walk all the way to school.

I used to go with my Aunty Glady all the time. Her and I would go and do weeding, she would always give me some money for helping her. I think this is why I don't mind doing weeding now and when I start I gotta keep going until I finished.

I blocked a lot of my memories out when I was young and on the reserve, and it's good that I am talking about my childhood now because things are coming back to me.

I was taken in 1963 when I was 12 years old and didn't come back until 1965. I was in Wandering mission for about a year. Then I was sent to Rossmoyne in Riverton because I did well at my schooling. I would come back to Wandering for holidays and it was good because I would see my sister Pat as she was still there.

So, this is my connection to York.

Sandra Narkle

Aaron Slater

My name is Aaron Slater. I am 34 years of age and live in York with my family. My grandmother, Sandra Narkle, lives here too. She is from here, and lived on the reserve with her mother – my great grandmother, Pauline Narkle née Kickett. So, York is home to me.

I like to do art with my daughter, Bree. She always comes and sits with me and together we create a painting. I have a couple of paintings that I will never sell, because these paintings are about country.

I moved away from home and lived in different places, but I came back home to sort myself out. I had to come home to York to heal. So yeah, I am home and continue to heal and stay strong for my family.

I grew up in York and went to school here. Growing up in York I remember old fellas telling us many stories. Mum and Nan Pauline often talked about the seven-footer. Some family members have seen him too. When I was little, we were told to git inside when it got dark cause that Moulie was outside waiting in the dark and he would git you. When I was older, I was told to be home before dark as the Moulie man was wondering around. Yeah, so, we had to be home before dark. Nanna Pauline used to say that to all of us kids as she didn't like us being outside after dark no matter what age we were.

My pop, Ross Narkle, he took me and my brother one day and we climbed the big hill, Walwaling. I didn't know at the time why we had to climb right to the top. When I got home, Nan Pauline told me why.

Aaron Slater

Bree Slater

My name is Bree Slater. I am 18 years old, and I live in York. When I was 12 years old, we came to stay with Nanna Sandra in York. Nanna Sandra used to tell us how she grew up on the reserve and about her family here in York. I then felt like York was home for me.

I did most of my schooling here at York. I started in Year 2 and went through to Year10. When Aunty Cathy had her house over on Cowan Road, we could see the big hill clearly. One day the boys decided to climb the big hill. They were told they had to climb it right to the top and if they didn't some one in their family would die. Jimmy my brother got tired when he was climbing, so one of the other boys piggy-backed him to the top. I remembered this when I heard the story of the two hills being read while we were practising for the play as part of The York Festival.

I really enjoyed doing the play for the festival, but I didn't like dancing in front of everyone. I got shame. But I got over it and managed to do my part. Mum and dad and Nanna Sandra came to watch the play, so it was good.

My connection to York is through my family.

Bree Slater

Gran's Pink and Grey Cocky

I remember when I was a little girl on the reserve. I used to go to my grandmother Blurton's house. Some family members called her Granny Jo. To most of us kids she was just Gran. Gran used to always be making us kids things like cakes.

Gran had two pink and grey cockies over some time. Some of us remember Gill and some of us remember Pete. I remember Pete always talking and telling Gran things like when the baker left the bread on the side of the road. Who was coming or asking who was here at Gran's house.

One day I looked towards the road and so did Gran's cocky Pete, who said: "Here comes Wally and he's drunk!" Then Pete looked again and said: "Bill, oh no, not Bill!" Then he turned upside down.

I looked to the road, and there was Uncle Wally staggering along and my father not far behind him.

Geraldine Metcalf née Blurton

Billy the Kid and his friend Sam

Billy Kickett and Sam Winmar taken on the York reserve
1947

Growing up in York I was told many stories by my
dad, George Kickett senior. Dad always referred to
his younger brother as Billy and I always called him
Uncle Billy or Uncle Nookar.

I asked dad why he called his brother Billy the
Kid sometimes. Dad started laughing and proceeded
to tell me why.

The following is the true story of Billy the Kid from York.

Billy the Kid had a best friend named Sam. He and Sam did everything together, even from a young age. They both loved going to the pictures and the best pictures were the cowboy movies. They loved John Wayne and Alan Ladd.

One day they saw a farmer using a handgun to shoot two stray dogs he had caught killing his sheep. The next day Billy the Kid, who after all was an outlaw, decided to walk into the farmhouse while the farmer's wife was hanging the washing on the line and take not one but two handguns, as well as bullets.

Doors were never locked in those days, as there was no need.

Up into the hills they went, as this looked like the country in a movie they had been to see. They loaded both guns and shared the remaining bullets.

Billy told Sam to make a run for it and started counting to 10. Sam headed for the hills, running as fast as he could, knowing Billy always started shooting before 10.

Sam ducked behind a rock just before the first bullet pinged off a rock nearby. Sam saw Billy running, so he fired at him but missed.

Sergeant Clifford was called by the farmer's wife

who saw Billy and Sam running from the house.

Sergeant Clifford was now down the bottom of the hill shouting at them, so they turned and started firing at him. The Sergeant kept shouting at them, but they couldn't see him, so they started shooting at each other again. They knew the Sergeant wouldn't be able to climb the hill to where they were.

The Sergeant continued shouting at them to come down.

Billy the Kid said he wasn't giving in.

Sam also shouted back, saying he was not giving in either. Eventually Billy and Sam fired all their bullets and were apprehended as they were reloading.

Tom Kickett was very strict and both boys got the hiding of their lives. No more going to the pictures. No supper that night.

As they lay on their sides, both agreed that they had the best time ever playing cowboys in the hills just out of York on the top Beverly Road. After such a hiding they understood how dangerous it was and were thankful to still be alive. They ate the food that was slipped out to them by big brother, George.

So that is why my dad called his younger brother Billy the Kid.

George Kickett senior, retold by Marion Kickett

The Brown Paper Bag

Billy Kicket taken in 1947 on the York Reserve

My name is Damon Metcalf Blurton Kickett. When I was a young kid my pop, Nookar Bill used to take us to the shop, and he used to buy us cool drink. We went back and told our mum, Geraldine, we used to say, "How come he buy us cool drink but his cool drink was in a brown paper bag all the time? How come ours weren't in a paper bag?"

My mum said, "Dad, what you taking them kids to the bottle shop for?"

He said, "Nah, nah, nah I never, never took them to the bottle shop. I brought 'em to the shop and bought 'em a cool drink."

"But they was telling me that yours was in a brown paper bag and theirs wasn't," she replied.

Yeah, we'd sit in the park by the river in Northam and drink our cool drink and he used to drink his out of the bag, but he never ever pulled it outta the bag, he never showed us what colour that bottle was in the brown paper bag. I thought he was drinking his cool drink.

But we used to tell on him all the time. Yeah! We used to dob him in all the time. We weren't dobbing on him for drinking, because as far as we were concerned, he was drinking cool drink like us, but we wanted the same a brown paper bag for our cool drink, the same as him.

He used to say to us, "Shut up or I am never taking you to the shop again."

That's one of the memories I have of my pop Nookar Bill.

Damon Metcalf Blurton Kickett

Saving a Monarch

My name is Jayden Metcalf, and I will tell you a story my dad told me about my great grandfather Pop Billy Kickett (Noonkar Bill), who is from York.

My Great Pop had a fine of $20. A monarch (policeman) came looking for him and saw him sitting in the park near the river. He started walking towards my Pop. My Pop saw him coming, so he jumped up and ran towards the river, with the monarch running after him. Pop dived into the river and started to swim to the other side. He didn't think the monarch would jump in the river as well, but he did. So, Pop started swimming faster and faster. He climbed up out of the river and sat on the riverbank catching his breath but keeping an eye on the monarch who was still swimming.

The river was running fast very fast and was high. Pop then saw the monarch, who was out in the middle of the river, sinking and coming up shouting. The monarch was drowning. So, my Pop dived back into the river and swam back to the monarch and helped him to the riverbank. My Pop saved that monarch's life. They didn't put my Pop in jail because he saved the monarch. They let him off for the $20 fine.

In this photo, (page 55) my Pop is standing by the river on the York reserve and the river is running. He was a hard worker. A fast bag sewer, a fast swimmer, and I am very proud of him.

Jayden Metcalf

The Cutter and the Bag Sewer

We are Jooken Nytte Koojal – "two little sisters".

We are 3 and 7 years old. We would like to share a story about our great pop – Billy Kickett.

We were told stories about our great pop. These stories were told to us by our dad. We would like to share this one story about how our great pop worked on the cutter.

Our great pop worked on the chaff cutter in York and Northam for many years. He used to sew the chaff bags.

We were told that our great pop was the fastest bag sewer ever. He used to sew the bags on the cutter. It was hard work and our great pop had to work in the hot sun all day long.

Many people in York remember our great pop. This makes us happy as we now live in York just like he did.

Allira and Alanie Metcalf

Merle Goodwin née Narkle

Gilgering

When I was five years old, we were staying on Mr Fred Fleay's farm near Gilgering. My grandfather Bernie Narkle camped near Gilgering siding. In the winter, I would pick field mushrooms in the paddock next to the Gilgering cemetery and church. Auntie Glady Narkle would cook the mushrooms up for us all to eat for a snack or with our meal. I would go with Auntie Glady across the river and walk to the farm - Oakover. Miss Fleay would walk down these stairs that went under the house. I was fascinated, watching her disappear down the stairs and then her head would appear and up she would come. I had never seen anyone walk down into a house before. Miss Fleay would come back with eggs and milk. I would then help auntie Glady carry the eggs and milk back to Grandfather where he had his camp at Gilgering.

I was born in 1947 and in 2021 I turned 74. I remember saying the numbers were now reversed. I was born in 47 and now I am turning 74. My sister Marion arranged for me to visit Oakover and as it turned out the visit was on the day, I turned 74. It was 69 years since I had been to Oakover. I remembered not being able to cross the river in winter as the river was running. As we drove across the river, I remembered crossing the river when I was five years old… such wonderful memories of so long ago.

Recently I caught up with Ron and Val Fleay and their daughter Caroline who came up from Perth. I met David Fleay and his wife Leslie their son Darcy and his wife. We had afternoon tea and Ron and I yarned about the old days. It was wonderful, as Ron remembered Grandfather Bernie and Grandfather Kenny Narkle and many others who used to live at Gilgering. I talked to David about his Grandfather Mr Fred Fleay. David showed me the old ledgers that his father and grandfather had kept, and I saw many of my family's names listed in the ledgers. Before we left, David helped me down the stairs and into the cellar of Oakover. It was so nice to go down into the cellar and have a look. Something that I had always wanted to do as a child. So here I was at 74 years of age being helped down the stairs and into the cellar by Mr Fred Fleay's grandson!

The York Reserve

I started school from the York reserve. I completed year 10 at the York high school and remember being told I was the first Aboriginal student to do so. Mum made it easier for me, as when I got older she bought me a bike. I used to ride my bike to school every day. Sometimes on the way home from school mum asked me to go to Mr Screigh's butcher shop and buy some meat which I would then take home and cook for our dinner. I remember using whatever I found in our little pantry cupboard. Mostly dry ingredients like pasta, split peas, pearl barley and packets of soup such as chicken or vegetable. This really helped Mum as the meat was fresh from the butchers and I saved her a lot of time. Mum was then able to make a damper to go with the stew that we had for dinner. My brothers and sisters all had jobs to do after school, but being older this was my job.

Merle Goodwin née Narkle

Back row left to right - Josephine Kickett, Zoe Hill, Merle Goodwin (nee Narkle)
Front row left to right - Irene Mills, Fred Kickett and Audrey Nettle (nee Narkle)
Taken on the York reserve 1960

Audrey Narkle Nettle

My name is Audrey Narkle Nettle. My mum was Pearl Brown Narkle Kickett.

I was born in August on the Moora Reserve in a tent in 1950. My mum said it was a very rainy night. Mum didn't go to the hospital, because back then there were aboriginal midwives who assisted when babies were born.

Mum also told me that my grandmother Grace Narrier was a midwife, but when mum was getting close to giving birth to me, grandmother went missing because she didn't want to be present for her daughter giving birth. I was born a very healthy 8-pound baby.

My husband Graham Nettle and I met on the York Reserve. When we met, he told me that he too was born on the Moore Reserve in a tent, however at the top end of the reserve. His mum was also assisted during his birth by the Aboriginal midwives. He weighed 10 pounds.

All I could say was, "Your poor mother".

I would like to share one of many stories about my time in York. My husband Graham and I were living in Hope Street, York, near my parents and younger siblings who lived on Cowan Road.

I was about six months pregnant with my second son Brendyn. I had my driving licence, and on many occasions mum and I, with my eldest son Trevor and sister Tracey, would go collecting wood. This day we were out on Ulster Road and the muffler fell off.

I said to mum, "We will have to wait until the muffler cools down and then I can put it back on." Mum looked at me in shock. We sat and waited for the muffler to cool down.

Tracey and Trevor said they needed to go to the toilet. Trevor went over to the fence, as boys do, and had a wee. Tracey asked where the toilet was, and mum tried to get her to squat. She was having none of that and kept saying, "Where is the toilet?"

She ended up having to wait. I then got the pliers out of the toolbox and went over to the nearby fence to cut off some wire. I then returned to the car. I laid down at the back end of the car and wired the muffler back on.

I then drove home, with mum still in shock.

Audrey Narkle Nettle

Three stories from George Kickett

The School Bus

We would catch the school bus (from Green Hills) to school each day from the reserve.

One day when coming home from school on the bus, the driver was just about to stop and let us off when my older sister got into an altercation with another girl.

The bus driver closed the door to find out what had happened then kicked all of us off the bus. When we got home, we told Mum what had happened.

Mum had a plan. The following day, she asked me and my cousin to get ready for school and go and wait at the bus stop. Mum told me if the bus didn't stop, I could stay home from school. My cousin was told the same. My mother thought the bus driver might stop for the two youngest children.

So, my cousin and I did what Mum said. As we watched the bus coming my cousin was saying – "Keep going, keep going, keep going" and the bus kept going. The bus driver would not stop for us. So, we stayed home that day and walked to school for the rest of the week, the distance being two miles.

I wondered why Mum made me and my cousin get ready for school and go wait at the bus stop. Thinking back, Mum had a plan.

This is where the welfare (people are) portrayed in a positive light. Mum knew the welfare were due to visit soon and they came the very next day to do their checks. They would check if there was anyone new living on the reserve, they would check our gardens, as well as if the toilets were clean and if all children were attending school.

Mum explained what had happened, including that she had asked her 7-year-old son to get ready for school and go and wait for the bus at the bus stop. Mum went on to explain that the bus driver wouldn't even stop for a 7-year-old. The welfare said they would talk to the headmaster and sort it out. And sort it out is what they did. We were allowed back on the bus the following Monday.

Getting our sister home safe and sound from the hospital

My sister Audrey had sprained her ankle while playing follow-the-leader and she of course was the leader. Audrey swung from a tree branch and landed awkwardly, spraining her ankle. Dr Ward kept her in hospital for a few days. Mum received word that Audrey was better, and she could come home. Fred and I were told to go to the hospital and help Audrey back home. We wondered how we were going to get her home. She wasn't to bear weight, was mums' words. We decided to take the old cane pram which we now used to collect wood.

We arrived at the old hospital, which wasn't far from the reserve, with the pram. Audrey asked us how we were going to get her home. Then she saw the old pram. Both Fred and I told her we weren't going to carry her home to the reserve. It was close but not that close. Audrey fitted in the pram but had her legs sticking out the end.

Very good at giving instructions Audrey started telling us what to do and how to do it on the road to the reserve. Yes, she was older than us, but we were here to help get her home. By the time we got to Mrs Sargent's house we had had enough. We looked ahead and made sure there were no cars coming and then we decided to let the pram run on its own down the slight hill. The pram started to build speed and we had to run to keep up we kept running alongside the pram which, in Fred's words, was now whistling along the road.

Audrey was screaming that she was going to kill me and Fred. Legs kicking and her screaming all the way as we guided the pam into the reserve.

Yes, we had gotten our sister home safe and sound from the hospital.

The Bag Sewers

I was working at the panel beaters in York and on the way home I stopped off at the Mill to pick up Dad and Uncle Bill. It was Friday and they were still sewing the last of the bags of chaff bought in from the paddocks. Everyone used to say they were entertaining to watch. They both had their own style of bag sewing. Dad's stiches where an inch apart, straight and tight. No chaff was going to fall out of his chaff bags.

Uncle Bill's stitches were also good but different to Dad's. Uncle sewed his bags with a different style. He ended his sewing with a fancy double-stitch and as he finished, he would raise his hand up in the air with flair. He certainly looked good, and he was fancy. On this day, when he finished he turned to dad and said, "You got speed, but I got style, my brother." Dad turned and replied, "I don't care what you got Billy; I beat you." Dad beat Uncle Bill by about 3-4 seconds. That's the memory I have of Dad and Uncle Bill sewing chaff bags on the York chaff cutter at the York Mill.

George Kickett

Back Row - Geroge Kickett Junior, Geraldine Metcalf (nee Blurton)
Middle Row - Verna Ford, Janice Kickett (York Janice Kickett)
Front - Rhonda Ronan (nee Blurton)
Taken on the York reserve 1959

A Story of Connection Belonging and Resilience

Photo taken on the York Reserve, 1963.
left – right: Marion Kickett, Darryl Narkle, Alana Narkle,
Ross Narkle and Len Blurton.

York is home. York has always been home, and York will always be home. I was born in the first spring known as Djiilba in York in 1962 on the veranda of the old hospital. This Noongar season is a combination of wet days with an increasing amount of clear cold nights and lovely warm days. My mum would always tell me I was born during shearing time. If the sheep were wet from the rains the lovely warm days would dry them out.

My dad was a shearer and I remember the smell of sheep's wool very well. It is still one of my most favourite smells. Why? Because I am reminded of how much we were all loved on the reserve in York. A place of serenity, connection and belonging, a place that was home.

I came home every day from school to the reserve and instantly felt happy even though I may not have felt happy at school that day. I had my gran, aunties, uncles, older cousins' younger cousins and of course mum and dad. Most people who came to the reserve were family and they would usually bring other people with them. Individuals or groups could not just turn up on the reserve they had to come there with someone or come to see someone they knew who lived on the reserve. People were always coming and going some stayed for a night or two while others stayed for weeks and months.

When I got older, I left York to pursue a career in nursing. During my training when things got tough, I would come home to regain my strength and then return invigorated and with an ability to meet challenges head-on. Never did I think about giving up or giving in.

Regardless of where I was living and working, I always came home to York for a day or several days and would always leave feeling energised, strong, and contented.

When I felt weak, I would come home to York to regain my strength. When I had a loss, I came home to grieve and mourn. When I felt sick, I came home to heal. When I felt tired, I came home to rest.

Whatever adversities or challenges I have had to face during my life, my resilience is due to having a strong sense of belonging and connection to the town of York in Barladong country. I am and will always be Barladong. It's where I belong.

Marion Kickett

Tracey Kickett

Taken at Cowan rd York 1972
Tracey Kickett (Tracey Kickett York) and
Trever Nettle

I have many special memories of growing up in
York, and I've chosen a few from when I was four
years of age and lived on Cowan Road...

Mushroom picking

Early on a Saturday morning Marion, Donna and myself would go mushroom picking in the paddock opposite our house. Dad used to ask the farmer Mr Marwick during the week if we could pick mushrooms in his paddock. Permission was always granted.

It was so much fun looking for field mushrooms. I learnt very quickly from Marion and Donna the difference between toadstools and mushrooms.

I remember running fast to jump the fence to get away from the ram chasing us. Marion and Donna cleared the fence and my black pants got hooked on the barbed wire. The ram ran at me twice and butted me in the backside. Marion and Donna looked like they were in shock and stood watching the ram butt me, until I yelled at them to get me off the fence. Donna ran and lifted me off the fence. We walked home with the bucket of mushrooms and ate them for breakfast. I love field mushrooms to this day.

Gilgering

At the same age I loved to go Gilgering with my older siblings down the river at the end of Cowan Road. I loved watching my sister Viv, brother Phil and brother-in-law Graham, put their hands into the side of the riverbank and pull out gilgies. Gilgies are smaller than marron and much sweeter than crayfish.

Unfortunately, there are not very many gilgies left in the York river today, as the river is quite sick now. I asked my older sister Audrey recently how my brother, sister and brother-in-law never got pinched on their hands by the gilgies when they pulled them out of the riverbank. She explained how they used to put the tips of their fingers and thumb together and make sure that lots of mud and clay was on them before putting their hands into the gilgies' burrow on the side of the river.

When we had enough gilgies for everyone in the bucket, we would go home and cook them. It was a real treat for everyone, they tasted so sweet. This would be our tea – fresh gilgies from the river.

Feather and Facey

Whilst living on Cowan Road my nephew Trevor, who is a year younger than me, lived behind us on Hope Street. We both could not pronounce the letter "T" in our names or any other word that started with T, so we used to call each other Feather and Facey.

We played with each other every day and had many adventures. One of our favourite adventures involved playing in an old broken-down truck across the road from Trevor's house. We used to take turns at driving this truck and pretend we were driving here or there. One day we went to climb into the truck windows either side and both of us spotted a tiger snake coiled up on the front seat. We both fell back out of the truck windows at the same time and landed on our backs. We got up and ran very quickly to Trevor's house and told his mum, my sister Audrey. We never played in that old truck again.

Not long after this incident with the tiger snake one of our male relatives was chased by another tiger snake around his car while we were picking dead wool in a paddock. All the kids jumped up on the roof of the car and our relative jumped up on the bonnet of the car and got rid of the snake.

Tina

I remember it was winter and my sisters Janice and Marion, niece Donna, and Mum and Dad were all in the lounge watching TV and we had a lovely warm fire. Mum went to sit on a seat, and I said, "Don't sit there, you will squash Tina". My Dad asked me who Tina was. I told him she was my friend. He asked what she looked like, and I described her: black hair, big brown eyes, my size, white nightie and that she was a *whajella* (white person). I remember telling Dad that she looked white. Dad then asked where she come from. I told him, down the road from the river (at the end of Cowan Road). (When I got older, I realised that Tina looked pale and obviously had drowned in the river; also, her nightie was an old style from settlement days).

From that evening on, everyone accepted Tina as my imaginary friend. Mum used to get really annoyed sometimes as I would ask her to pick up Tina and put her in her shopping bag during our walk to town, as Tina was tired. Mum would say, "This Tina! You the one getting tired, not Tina!" I would assure her that it was Tina and not me.

If you have ever watched the movie "Drop Dead Fred" about an imaginary friend or even had an imaginary friend, you would know how they can get you into a lot of trouble.

Mum was doing the washing one day, and I was playing on the front verandah making mud pies. Tina came along and wanted to play. Tina started throwing the mud pies all over the inside of the verandah. I begged her to stop as I knew Mum would get angry with me because of the mess. Mum came around from the back to check on me and seen the mess. I got the biggest hiding ever and Tina was so sorry that she got me in trouble and promised to never do this again. My sister Audrey washed the verandah down with the hose and calmed Mum down.

We moved to Grey Street just before I commenced school, and I didn't see Tina again until I was an adult living in Tuart Hill. Tina appeared and looked quite stressed. She was now an adult like me, and I realised later that she had come to give me a warning about something quite traumatic that would happen for me soon.

Tracey Kickett

Montanna Rose Miller

I have never lived in York but have a strong connection to this little old town. I have visited York many times with my great grandmother Vivienne Narkle (RIP). Nan would take me to York for holidays especially when she wanted to come to what she called home for a break from the city. Nan wanted us kids to know where eggs and milk came from.

We spent time on a farm where we collected the eggs, but I just couldn't touch the teat of a goat or cow to squeeze the milk out. I also remember my bladder nearly bursting because I wouldn't go to the toilet out in the bush. Nan was disgusted with us, calling us "city kids".

I was raised by my grandmother Donna Narkle (RIP) who was raised in turn by her grandmother Nanna Pearl Kickett (RIP), who my aunty Tammy Miller always called Nanna York.

I remember when I would get home, I would tell Mum Donna (RIP) all about York. I told her about this bridge that would swing. The lookout on the hill and how you could see the whole town. I told her about the old jail that had lots of Noongars' names on the wall and one of them was Nanna Viv's (RIP) uncle Rusty Narkle (RIP). I told her how we walked around the big old school and sat in this very old lunch shed where Nanna Viv (RIP) used to eat her lunch at school, and we bounced a netball around on the court. Lastly, I told her that we swam in the swimming pool nearly every day as it was so hot.

Mum Donna (RIP) would look at me and smile then say, "Yes, I know." I would say to her "No! you don't, you haven't been to York with us on holidays." Mum Donna (RIP) then told me that she didn't need to go to York for holidays because she grew up in York, went to school in York and she too sat in that old lunch shed and ate her lunch. Both Nanna Viv and Mum Donna have passed. I come to York to remember them both.

When I was asked to be a part of the play Two Mountains Dreaming for the 2022 York Festival I never hesitated. I felt proud to play Wilurah, whose spirit was sent to Wongborel which means "Sleeping Woman".

I did this for the two women who raised me together my great grandmother Vivienne Narkle and my grandmother Donna Miller née Narkle.

Montanna Rose Miller

My connection to York, which like my Mum is where I belong

I have always come to York with my mum. She would show me where she lived and went to school. She told me about the swing bridge, and the two hills. The woman's hill and the man's hill. I was also taken to where the reserve was many times, and I feel privileged to be able to see Nanna Pearl's and Great Gran Josephine's photos of the reserve in theirs and my mums' days.

I love looking at the old photos of Nan Pearl and Pop George because I never knew them. Also the photos of aunties Jan and Viv, uncle Phil, my cousins Donna, Todd and Do boy photos taken on the reserve in York. Such memories make me very happy and a connection to York.

Mum told me the story of how she and Donna my cousin would go to the Chinese market garden when they were little, age 4 and 5, and buy watermelons with the pennies my pop gave them. Mum said Donna would always drop her watermelon so she could eat it right then and there. She didn't want to wait until she got home to have a feed of watermelon. Mum said the old Chinese man was very kind and always gave Donna another watermelon to take home, only this time he carried the watermelon to the car for her.

Mum still has some coins: a penny, a shilling a threepence, one cent, two cents and a round 50 cents. She also has a dollar note, which is brown, and a two dollar note, which is green. Mum told me this is the kind of money her and Donna used in York when they were little.

When I was about five years old, Mum and I were walking along the river with Aunty Merle and Aunty Jan. I started to scream and jump around. Mum saw the baby tiger snake the same time as me and in one swoop picked me up out of harm's way. Aunty Merle hunted the little snake towards the river while Auntie Jan had run up towards the bridge and was yelling at us to move away as there might be more baby snakes – and their mother. At school on Monday, I told my class about the snake and stretched the truth just a bit. I told the class that my Aunty Merle had grabbed the snake and broke its neck.

Whilst crossing the swing bridge one day with

Mum and Aunty Audrey and Aunty Merle, Aunty Audrey told me how Uncle Phil had bought her a camera. She said Aunty Merle had taken the camera and whilst taking photos on the swing bridge she had dropped the camera in the river. Aunty Merle said that the camera had slipped out of her hands, and it was all an accident. I don't believe that Aunty Audrey thought or believed this is what happened. I am not too sure what had happened, after all I wasn't born. Mum couldn't help me either as she was just a baby at the time or maybe not there either. So, this is a mystery and remains a mystery. But every time I cross the swing bridge, I think about my two aunties and the camera. I also wonder if that camera is there on the bottom of *Bilya Googala* (Avon River).

Although my mum and I have now bought a house in York, I always believed we had a big house in York where a lot of people stayed. Mum used to say these people were allowed to stay there. They ate breakfast where we ate breakfast but like me and mum had their own rooms. We all could eat toast, cereal, and yogurt. I would drink orange juice. Mum could make tea or coffee. The people staying with us could as well.

As it turned out, we spent many weekends in York and would stay at the Castle Hotel.

Pearle Kickett

Nyingarn (Echidna)

I have a good memory of when Mum and I found a *nyingarn* (echidna) in our backyard. It was digging, and we watched it do this digging. My mum told me that our family (Kickett) spirit animal is the *nyingarn*. They belong to the Wongborel Hill (Mt Brown), the "sleeping woman". It is our job to look after the *nyingarn* and they will look after us too.

Jo' Cassius Shea

Walking together on Country

Spoken by Marion Kickett and heard by John Kinsella who responds

Marion Says:

Let's walk together on country right now and look to see what there is to see. Wongborel (Mt Brown), Walwalling (Mt Bakewell) and Bilya Googalar (Avon River in York) too. Within my view is a Yongka or two (Kangaroo), a weitj (Emu) and Nyingarn (Echidna) but only a few.

Ballay (lookout), something running fast, too fast for me to see. Ah it's a karda (Lizzard) a Karda running way over there. Look, look again is that a numbat messin around? He chasin ants, ants, everywhere his sucking them up he don't care.

It's been raining and raining what do you smell? The dampness of boodja (land) and the Eucalyptus trees, the aroma of Bilya Googalar (river) running fast further over there.

Nih Nih (Listen, listen) what's that you hear? Its Wardong (crow) and Kulbardi (magpie) talking somewhere over there as they sit watching Djidi Djidi (Willy Wagtail) play just there.

So, come with me and let's walk on country the way my ancestors did. Let's listen and see what we can see and learn as we walk on country.

John Responds:

I walk on your country, Marion, and say thanks. I see
    the river and the mountain and the hill
    and I hear their names.

I walk on your country, Marion, and am grateful.
    I hear the Yongka through the undergrowth
    and hear Nyingarn shuffling to its fallen
    tree-trunk hollow.

But I am sad I can't see the numbats as you know
    them, Marion, because they've been driven
    away.

I walk on your country, Marion, and listen to your
    words. I too hear the Djidi Djidi having its

say, playing with the times of day.

I walk on your country, Marion, and also see the
heron looking beyond its reflection in Bilya
Googalar. What's the heron's name,
Marion?

I will follow where you lead, Marion, and learn
as I go. I will listen and learn. I will feel
the ground under my feet, the sky overhead,
hear the river flow.

Marion Says:

The word for heron John that is most common to
use is bull – ong, John. That's the word my dad used.

Feeling and Healing, Country.

Now that we have walked together on country just
now, let us see how we can heal our country heal this
country right now. But first we must listen and listen
to learn if we are to work together, we must listen to
earn. The benefit of knowing what happened long
ago, is important for you to learn and then to know.

In 1831 my people had heard, they had heard
your people coming, and coming they were, not far
now, not far now, just a little further a little further

right now. They were heard they were heard they were heard just now.

Nih Nih (Listen, listen) what's that they are saying? What's that they got? what is it they want? Ahh, it is our water they want, and not just for them, for the animals too and some more to carry could this be true? Yes, it's true it must be true, as they are not many just a few.

As time went by my people showed your people the way, they showed your people they showed them the way. We worked together your people and mine working together on country was fine. We cared we shared but not for long. Your people were different as they wanted to own. We don't own country we belong we belong, and we have belonged to country for so, so long. We look after country for so long for so long. Your people damaged my country, and it didn't take long.

Misunderstanding, Misunderstandings. My people did not understand why your people came to their land, why they took their land. They believed you came in peace and shared with you not just their land, but their knowledge too. Where to find water and where to fish, where to hunt and how not to miss, yes, my people showed your people everything, everything as they had wished.

They watched your people build houses they

watched as they built their barns. They watched more of your people coming more people coming to build farms. Your people building their homes, growing their food my people started to be rude. They burnt your people's crops houses too also speared a sheep or two.

In 1833 the blood of both our peoples began to spill and spill until 1835 but we survived yes, we survived. In 1836 my people's blood run quick, it was running on country so, so quick. In 1837 my people's blood was soaking it was soaking our country I feel sick I feel so sick.

John Responds:

I know all you say is true, Marion, and I grieve for
         its truth.
I know all you say is true, Marion, and I want to help
         redress.
I know all you say is true, Marion, and I want to learn
         better how to share.
I know all you say is true, Marion, and won't pretend
         this isn't history.
I know all you say is true, Marion, and I am hoping
         to understand how it happened and how we
         can find the peace and let spirits rest
         in peace and learn that knowledge

isn't something just to be stolen but to say
thanks for and use as we're supposed to use
if we're to use it at all, and give something
back not just take and take and take.
I know all you say is true, Marion, and I want to
respect the blood-soaked earth I want
the river to flow as it flowed and as it
should flow I want to follow your trail
and know the country as you would have me
know it, as you show me I know all you say
is true, Marion, and I want the history books
to be rewritten to tell the truths you tell
and not to try and reword it also excuses
are made when settlers can't make excuses
but must face up to the truth and try to make
things right even if things can't be made
right because so much wrong has been
done — try to make right because
that's what we have to do through
generations and generations of wrong.
I know all you say is true, Marion, and sorry is not
enough — I vow to work to help bring
change to restore country to let the river
tell us rather than we tell it to listen to your
knowledge and respect your knowledge
to respect and protect the sacred places
to hear the stories and look back to how

we came here and what we have to do
to bring peace to country.
I know all you say is true, Marion — from
Walwalinj to Wongborel, as the river
flows between and the birds and animals
and river creatures confirm the stories
and I follow you across country,
the salinity retreating back into the ground
and the wattles flowering with truth.
I am hoping we can work together, Marion.
I am hoping we can stand by the river
and share words.
I am hoping you can trust what I say Marion.
I know all you say is true. I am listening. I am
seeing.
I am learning.

Marion Says:

So let us together remember the past and together
we must bring it, bring it with us and make it last.

Let's acknowledge the mistakes that occurred
back then and work together so together we can
learn.

My country has been desecrated of this we both
know so let's work together yes let's give it a go.

When we walk on country what do we see? I see
terrible things; terrible things are what I see.

I see rubbish, rubbish is what I see. Left right there on our beloved country.

White goods and furniture, trolleys too. I see old machinery rusting near, because its far more convenient to dump it here.

I wonder why people let their cats run on country, run on country as they do. I ask you John what must we do what must we do?

John Says:

We must gather and talk with each other, Marion,
      about the best way through.
We must listen to the Elders and respect what they
      tell us — I must listen to you.
We must not hide from the truth. We must not
      let the last fragments of bush
      disappear.
We must join those fragments of bush together
      and hope the numbats might return.
We must let the splendid fairy wrens find their way
      through the seasons and bring blue out of
      eclipse. We must never let go, we must
      never give in.
We must respect country and not rubbish
      and exploit it.
We must respect country and let it heal through

learning and heal through doing. I hope
we can work together.

I follow you across your country, Marion,
and hope I can learn, too.

I am willing, Marion... I am willing to do the work.

Marion Says:

Come gather all of you and let us talk of the best way
forward and so then we can walk. As it's not just
about talking but walking too as there is so, so much
to do.

Let's listen to the elders, together let's listen to
them, so we may all hear, hear what is said. Together
let us all show respect and listen to learn for there is
much so much to earn.

Walk with us and feel country and learn as we do
on our country. Kneel next Bilya Googalar and feel
kep (water) running, running through our country.

It is wise, yes, it is wise for all of us to try not to
hide. Listen to the history, acknowledge it, and
accept. Because it is a history we cannot forget.

Come with John and me and lets all work
together to see. We must not let the last of our bush
disappear this is something we fear oh dear, oh dear.

We must join those fragments of bush together
and hope our numbats return forever.

We must never let go, we must never give in.
Let's all work together to repay the last sins.

If we share our knowledge which is real yes, it is
real, and work together and help our country to heal.

Acknowledgments

The York Festival would like to acknowledge all who have assisted with this project, including the generous support of Ian Hooper and his team at Leschenault Press/The Book Reality Experience and Healthway/Act Belong Commit.